I0134222

How Things Tasted When We Were Young

poems by

Nadra Mabrouk

Finishing Line Press
Georgetown, Kentucky

How Things Tasted When We Were Young

ACKNOWLEDGMENTS

Thank you to the editors of the following publications in which some of these
poems first appeared, often in earlier forms: *22 Magazine, Strange Girl Press, Thin
Air Magazine, Jai-Alai, RHINO, Print-Oriented Bastards, The Boiler Journal, The
Grief Diaries,* and *Origins Literary Journal.*

Special thanks to Peg Boyers, Campbell McGrath, Julie Marie Wade, and Cindy
Chinelly for their inspiring mentorship. And to Marci Calabretta Cancio-Bello
and Ariel Francisco for their loving attention to the poems in this chapbook.

Thanks to my parents, Usam Mabrouk and Hemat Waziry, and my siblings,
Mohamed, Walid, and Naglaa, for their support. And to my grandparents, Nadra
Elsayed and Mustafa Waziry.

Publisher: Leah Maines

Editor: Christen Kincaid

Cover Art: Nadra Mabrouk

Author Photo: Diana Buitrago

Cover Design: Elizabeth Maines

Printed in the USA on acid-free paper.
Order online: www.finishinglinepress.com
also available on amazon.com

Author inquiries and mail orders:
Finishing Line Press
P. O. Box 1626
Georgetown, Kentucky 40324
U. S. A.

Table of Contents

For Zain

May you build a ladder to the stars
And climb on every rung

—Bob Dylan, "Forever Young"

Where does unbelief begin?
When I was young

there were degrees of certainty.
I could say, Yes I know that I have two hands.
Then one day I awakened on a planet of people whose hands occasionally
disappear—

—Anne Carson, "The Glass Essay"

Crooked

When I take my sister down
to see the Nile in December, she will close
her hands, clench her fingers, whisper
her closed breath down onto her wrists
in the air billowing through the hour.

And there, I will hold her the way only
an older sibling can,
want to push her into it : slowly
whispering something like *don't look back,*
you are here,
remembering our mother in the bathroom,
pearl-mouthed, separating her own thinning hair
into sections for the red dye
(the color of flesh, a brain split in half),
say while her gloved hands dug into her bald spot,
when someone is bipolar
it means a part of their brain is crooked.
Her voice—a merciless blue current.
And my sister looked at me, gap in teeth,
not understanding, lopsided.

By the river, we will step on the soil like mesh,
thick pockets of fertility, unpacked bodies of plume thistles,
imagining still, slender, dead fish lining the riverbank,
rolling back into the water when we accidentally kick them.

My hands will press on her upper arms,
her thick hair will weigh less here, float, the torn
ends split in twos and threes will fall
away set free from her scratched scalp.
And when the tilapia swim past her once heavy frame,
moving together and never parting—one grey body,
fringed gold and pink at the tips,

her shriveling body: yellow, effusive, will spread out.
She will empty
into the Mediterranean, something larger
encompassing her body, her spine slightly curved,
her head: waterlogged.

Maturing

Your fingers make holes
where the chrysanthemums sprouted, lopsided
at first, then more rigid
but still soft
enough to pull apart.

You do this before dawn, when no one else can
hear over the static wash of the sprinklers—
pull each one out and throw it

to the side, deformed petals
already releasing their center, falling.

I thought to hold your wrist down, sink
your hands into the loam,
bury each finger permanently until you are crippled
by the hunger of the earth,
to say you shouldn't. But I watch you dig
out each one. I sit by the pile,
tightening
my grip over each anther.

Letter from the Nile
to Leliegracht Canal, Amsterdam
   for S.

Lily, your full name sits in my mouth—rocks along the riverbank.
If I were from another continent, one that is charcoal, sleek-mouthed,

I would've been able to say it. But I only
know the tongue of conquerors, the curves of the Arabic alphabet

as the vowels curl into each other like hooks into flat palms, blemishes,
little foreign birth marks, dots in the rounded bellies of polished letters.

At night, the lanterns by the hotels make you glow. I stretch
each end of myself, empty into the Mediterranean Sea,

feel the water in my spine crack me at the edges,
wonder how old I've become. And you, tranquil and small,

lap quietly against every few boats
as they flow through underneath the bridge.

Concrete slab on concrete slab close off your curves
and you run straight down.

Lilly, tell me again in Amsterdam how the children
walk beside you, each small and white

and with a neon backpack, small fingers laced into each other,
fingernails with bits of grass underneath.

I imagine that couple
that come to stare at you from the bench, his shoulders tan and wet,

her eyes: grey, little. She will soon be far away from him.
I already hear her spelling out goodbyes,

scratching out some words, stumbling,
running her thin fingers through you.

The men still fish here. Their feet flat and hard
on the ground, large like their ancestors. I remember them too,

embalming their ill-lit insides as though they'll see
one another again. Now the fishermen throw

the line that feels like thread needling into me,
all the cat and tiger fish swarm like an oppressed mob

and one will bite, grip on the metal and the small spear
will pierce the roof of its mouth and it will still

hold that same, stunned expression on its face,
its body going into fits, sending orbs of pressure through

and the school will keep moving
a little more quickly this time, for a second—safe.

Stone Fruit

We pick from separate trees.
The plums leave our palms,
drop into the baskets at the same time.
In this end of summer, your skin glows:
glaucous, a halo of ash,
dead skin on each cheekbone.
Your mouth a thin line
showing only your teeth
when a few of the dark fruits topple from the branches.
I follow you through the orchard,
my basket lighter than yours,
birds pecking
at the mulberry trees,
your footsteps heavy, as though coated
with the fruit's wax.
Dropping all the soft plums from your arms,
two miss the basket. You stare at the stray spheres,
imagining the sour skin,
peeling it with your teeth,
the bitten insides that discolor so quickly.

Things I Couldn't Crack Open in My Mouth

I hold you with limp fingers,
body curled in my palms,
leaves cracking beneath
my sneakers' soles: small, wreathed ribcages lining the gravel.

Before this, the other parakeets were perched
on the artificial branch
chirping in between bites,
flower seeds dropping
like unhinged beaks, millet shells falling
lightly on your slit body.

The birds could cut their throats
with the calls. Within your bleeding cleft
that which is unsung,
in the open trachea—grit, fractured seeds.

I stare at the placid chest,
the white-footed ants already gathering.
Nerves flock—my knees and elbows bend to the run,
dependent on the unbearable restraint of bone to bone to bone.

Entrances

1.
June to June, I wish the air were wetter
pushing into and impregnating ponds.

In one photograph,
you're holding two slabs of yellow wood
to build a kitchen table for her.
In another, you are near a still lake,
thin, broken branch in hand pointing at nothing.
In the last, you are not yet conceived
but you exist in your father's eyes,
a small body already forming on the lips of the mother:
pink and thick and wanting.

2.
Always in the gangly outdoors,
I am almost without you.
On a long pathway,
you try to disappear
and I do not allow you.

At the last picnic
I imagined us as something near gray,
your chin shriveling
at the red pulp underneath my nails
sweetening the lines on my palms,
but I still picked
the wounded strawberries off the dripping wood.

Fingers dangling like sap,
you refuse to touch.

3.
In any war,
you would be the first
to be shot.

You: lingering and light haired.
Everyone sees you
threading everywhere like white skin,
like blonde, small hairs in hidden places.

In a warzone
where sweat-softened, brown heads
crack off, rolling like barrels,
you look around for me and I am no where near you.

4.
You pant with thirst,
a shrinking ice cube on your curled tongue.
It's good enough reason
to put your half of the sheet on me
and sidle farther away.

I survey your bare knees in the heat.
Our bodies are of no use.

Bracing for Impact

My sister is the flight attendant unfamiliar
with the safety procedures of the plane.

She stands between the rows,
holding the brochure over her head,

strawberry-eyed, chin still curled in
since she was 17 months. I sit

in 3A, watching her fumble, her eyes one moment
on the ironed-navy of the other flight attendant,

the next—the emergency exit.
She takes a few steps back, sways with the plane's

jagged preparations to take off. Later, somewhere
perhaps between two belts of countries where it is morning now,

a sister takes her scarf off in a sleek city, wraps it around
the soft skin on the collar bones of her sibling.

Or now, maybe over Bali, she is going through miles
of rice fields, the shallow paddies near her ankles, her bare feet

no longer dry. Maybe over Ghana now, she takes food
from her sister's fingers, eats it, apologizes she was born.

It is morning. My sister is walking up and down the plane's aisle,
holding an open carton of orange juice, her eyes on all the windows.

Memoir of Space

The ground, barely touched, an entire
field to cultivate—rain-wet miles
of new soil.
I have tried to create landmarks
for us to return to:
the wood splinters
my palms,
my fingers dangle over the ringed
brown of the unmarked, the still unmade.

You exist in movement,
furnishing a permanent home
somewhere above Ocala. The St. John's
flowing slowly North.

I take care of the expanse,
counting each bracelet of bone
in the ruddy spine through the state.

Freshwater

You wanted to use a caterpillar as fish bait.
The soft fuzz of its pinky-long body
squirmed as though in slow motion
and you, not able to cut into its mouth, shivering,
threw it back in the grass.

And I thought we could take this bike anywhere.
Instead, we stop,
lay it on the ground near my chalky ankles.

A half naked woman's shoulders near us, tanner than us—she is a bear
waiting for the small gloves of fish
to tug, then grabbing them off the hook with large fingers
and swollen palms
as though her growth depended on them.

And what does our growth depend upon?
Exoskeleton? Thin needles inside fish?
The sturdiness of understanding the variations of the skeletal system?

I turn to prickling hairs on your thin-skinned elbow
and rub my cheek against your ribs.
You place your fingers on the sinking earth of my face
as though tracing hunger on the cheekbone
as the woman limps away.

She leaves with a basket of fresh bodies.
Something to slice open, squeeze lemon on,
cradle in your mouth and feel whole.

In a thought made of silk,
I am cutting softened peaches into puddles of vanilla,
a dessert after salting the center of a cut salmon:
pink tongues on a refrigerated platter.

After we eat, a marinated silence
and hands smelling of the river,
something swift to salvage us.

But instead,
you fill your hands with the grainy metal of the handlebars
and walk ahead of me,
footsteps slow and dry in the heat.

Crescent

The Friday afternoon call to prayer
steadies the entire city for seconds

before it trembles again with the hurried footsteps.
The women tighten on their small children's hands,

their floral dresses trailing behind
taking small gravel of the city with them.

Every mother's son in the street, ready to pray while protesting,
every husband off today. The teenage girls leave their books at home,

wrap temporary shawls on their dyed hair
(light browns like the architecture, reds like their small thighs at night).

The minarets glow with the sunlight, the mosaics
in the glass make sunlit shapes on the pavement.

My mother is dressing for her prayer. Her once thick knees now crescents
waiting to wax again towards wholeness as the call echoes and floats,

the muezzin's voice circling the vowels
hangs on to one before singing of the other,

wraps around the pillars of the minarets,
combs the zipping streets, his tongue the only instrument.

Today my mother is too tired to walk through the streets
to go to prayer. Her knees crack, comminute when she takes any step,

each tick of her joints takes her closer
to the prayer playing on television,

I watch her blessings, whispering to clouds
I cannot see, stars floating to touch her

wrinkling face, taking her by her moon-shaped knees,
her shining forehead. The call ends, the prayer begins.

The shops all closed, everyone either in this mosque or the other,
in unison. My mother, cradling her fragility,

watches the cosmic emptiness from the window
then puts the volume up.

Virgin

a.
Imagine us before.
We opened the window and the air met us
as a wild animal set loose would.

It stretched out its cramped legs in front of us
and your sister's arms clung around my neck
as though she wished for me all of her days.
Her cheeks' curves red and wet.

b.
Under an Australian Pine,
we remember not belonging:
the sickness of roots and origins.

c.
Bellybuttons do not swell in response.
Yours does not swell between my large legs.
But we are careful where we touch.
It's the difference between biting and swallowing.

d.
Rubbing, I harass fragility.
Red is reliable.
Don't you itch, curving around a close-legged religion?

e.
I've never embraced God,
but I imagine how a deer's underbelly would feel.
And isn't this where we stab?

f.
A pillow.
Our knees meet over it as though hunger could save us.
I have dolls near the window.
My childhood's legs split open, free.

g.
If I were a jar,
I'd choose to encase limbless emptiness
not you.

h.
You say we are meant to eat animals.
Don't you miss how things tasted when we were younger
like your sister?
There is a milkiness to everything now,
orbs of groggy chicken embryos
make our hands move away from the plates in reluctance
and under.

i.
Inside stretches.

Cloven

Two gray sheep can only live so long
in your kitchen.

Your father, uncle, and grandfather
drag the two sheep past the hallway.
Holiday dinner breathes
and smells of wet wool.

Mother takes you to be bathed with your sister.
Together, you sit cross-legged
in the hot water
and you, while washing her hair,
start speaking.
Her small head meets your palms

and your nails are too short to scratch into the scalp.
You hold the small flow of urine inside of you
before it changes the color of the water
and ask her whether she knows why the sheep are here.

She shakes her head
and your lower stomach fat folds in weakness
to control the bladder.

You imagine your sister and yourself in their place
feeling your neck pretending your hand
were as thick as the butcher's.

They're going to kill them when the butcher is here.
You say *tradition*, mispronouncing it
but say it as a little urine slips out,
not enough to change the water.

Hooves start gnawing into the floor,
their bleating breathless
as though calling to apologize
for never watching over each other.

You run out and back into the bedroom
where it is warm. The blood
never reaches this far
but you imagine the pulp of it,
their open mouths, the small
square teeth of a toddler.

The Net

You pick up a stick, jabbing it into the thick puddle
of jellyfish melting into warm sand watching it shiver back into stillness.

You tell me that soon it will evaporate; by tomorrow
when we take the same walk along the shore, it won't be there anymore.

We stand there staring at it,
speaking eventually, our mouths full of salt,

before a sea stretch we can only imagine: underwater
caves full of colorless fish

(their gaping mouths—)
hundreds of species neither of us will ever see.

We speak of the possibilities that ruined them,
perhaps a tuna fishing vessel, yes, something vast

and heartless. A purse-seine net snapping
shut and we imagine them swimming,

an entire school of tuna, and maybe
these jellyfish floating into the net,

venom twitching at the tips of their tentacles
when their entire bodies were flashing, distant stars in the fog of the sea,

tentacles of water, swirling in water,
barely distinguishable in their bubbling movements, their light weight.

Here, the baggy lumps melt
at our also-shriveling feet.

You toss the stick into the water,
your heavy hand tries to comb through the tangles of my hair

as we watch it float back and forth,
our bodies still uncaught.

We Sleep Like Insects Covered in Old Sugar

We dreamt of the massacred—
how they ate before, fingers pinching holes in the bread.
Every night, we tried to end it prematurely,
to dismantle the curled insides of the children.
Tonight I am trying to figure out
which to pull on—blue or red?

Here

You leave
the suitcases in the old house of *Zamalek*
back in Cairo
and walk out where the dogs wag their bony tails
begging for food you don't have.

Once, you dropped
a bag of sugar when you were younger
and just kept running
wondering if it will melt on their tongues,
move like hot syrup down their throats,
if there's anything in it that might keep them alive.

Here in Cairo, what has kept you alive
and away?

Not quiet, not pure,
not seething nor starved
like the protesters of Tahrir Square,
their chests always open
to the city of a thousand minarets.
But entirely blank, scattered,
thin body of a minute hand of a clock
looking now at the homes of the past, the city's frail,
watered down brown, the color like the dirt
near the Nile, downtown Cairo, the rough wheels
of the *Fakahany's* fruit cart
on the uneven pavement, slapping the mule,
the legs of sheep as they bleat by,
their wool as thick and curled
as your brother's head next to you in bed
when he would wake you.

What woke you after that—the promise
of a warmed apple, small as your palm to sink
into? You'll remember your grandfather
and how he lived off of a watermelon cart,
spitting seeds into his hands
and smearing them off to the ground.

You walk down the streets of *Shobra*,
where each store is playing a separate song,
where your brothers' soccer ball was tattered
but still kicked around,
where the small boy ran after you only to tug
on your braid and run off.

You will remember your mother
using old shirts to wipe the floors
and the beggars stopping by the house
and how she would give them pounds of fresh meat and prayers:

I hope He will make you see again
or, *Your children are far*
but safe, full. I know.

Nadra Mabrouk grew up in Miami, FL where she earned a Bachelor of Arts in English from Florida International University. Her work has appeared in *Best Teen Writing of 2010*, published by The Alliance for Young Artists & Writers, *RHINO*, *The Boiler Journal*, and elsewhere. She is co-founder of Orange Island Review and an editor for *Jai-Alai Magazine*.

www.ingramcontent.com/pod-product-compliance
Lightning Source LLC
LaVergne TN
LVHW091236080426
835509LV00009B/1299